Tower Hamlets College
Learning Centre

D0545454

BOP BOP BOP

FLY BY NIGHT
THE NEW ART OF THE CLUB FLYER

CRAIG McCARTHY

This book is to be returned on or before
the last date stamped below or you will be
charged a fine

7 DAY LOAN

1 8 NOV 2009

1 1 MAR 2010

LEARNING CENTRE
TOWER HAMLETS COLLEGE
POPLAR HIGH STREET
LONDON E14 OAF
Tel: 020 7510 7765

Thames & Hudson

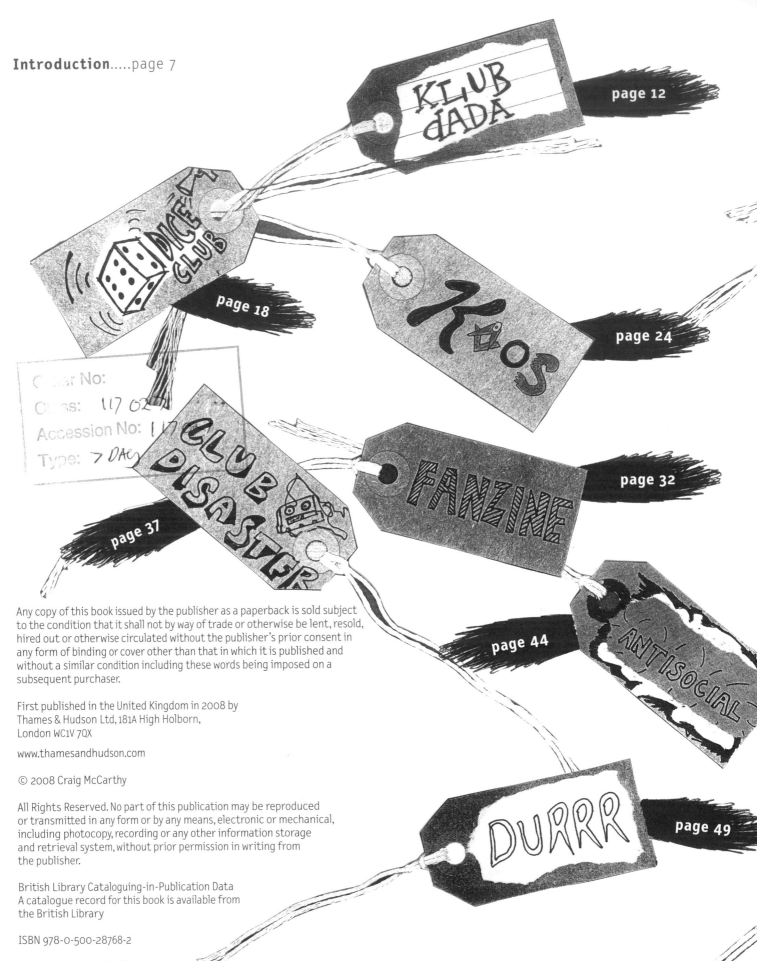

O der No:

C ss: 117 02

Accession No: 1

Type: 7 DA

Any copy of this book issued by the publisher as a paperback is sold subject to the condition that it shall not by way of trade or otherwise be lent, resold, hired out or otherwise circulated without the publisher's prior consent in any form of binding or cover other than that in which it is published and without a similar condition including these words being imposed on a subsequent purchaser.

First published in the United Kingdom in 2008 by
Thames & Hudson Ltd, 181A High Holborn,
London WC1V 7QX

www.thamesandhudson.com

© 2008 Craig McCarthy

All Rights Reserved. No part of this publication may be reproduced or transmitted in any form or by any means, electronic or mechanical, including photocopy, recording or any other information storage and retrieval system, without prior permission in writing from the publisher.

British Library Cataloguing-in-Publication Data
A catalogue record for this book is available from the British Library

ISBN 978-0-500-28768-2

Printed and bound in China by
SNP Leefung Printers Ltd

Fly By Night:

All mine, these pieces of night-time.

On my table are ten years' worth of scrapbooks. They are memorials to past nights, clubs and gigs, and repositories of flyers that I have accumulated since I was a teenager. Looking at the material, I can see cellars full of party monsters, hand-drawn inky pirates, fleshy vampires devouring fleshy victims, unskinny boppers.

I have hundreds of them, small oblong bits of paper – they are windows into other worlds: B-movies, dead stars, The Death Star, a white rabbit, an unfurling doodle, all of them weighing down my trestle table.

Each flyer tells me about a time and a place: stacked together they make a shape and form a visual diary. I shall keep them forever as they will tell me about now, then.

The flyers have become an obsession. Each week I make a trawl at my regular haunts just before dawn, knowing that I'll make a fresh catch. Many are decorated with drawings: artwork that is hand made, chance made, re-made, machine made, traced, copied, reflected, repeated. I hook them and stuff them into my pocket.

If I could have my way, I would make these flyers, which are so ephemeral and easy to throw away, immortal. Bits of paper, postcards and images have always intrigued me. I net them and ferociously glue each one down in a scrapbook.

This book is of the flyers that I have collected over the years. Incredible time spent in London – my friends, my books and brilliant nights.

Virginia
Creepers
Club

· AN ·
EVENING
FOR
MUSO - FO⊙
BOOZOIDS

⚜

FRI 12th
AUG

⚜

IMMORAL
MINORITY

18th October
DEBUT GIG
Supporting :
GOD, Bile Duct,
KADT,
Local Mad Man
The Old Kings Head
382 Holloway Road

DADA

KLUB KLUB KLUB KLUB KLUB KLUB KLUB KLUB KLUB KLUB KLUB KLUB

1 APRIL 2006

MAd GEORGE TAVErNE 373 cOMMERCIAL RD E1

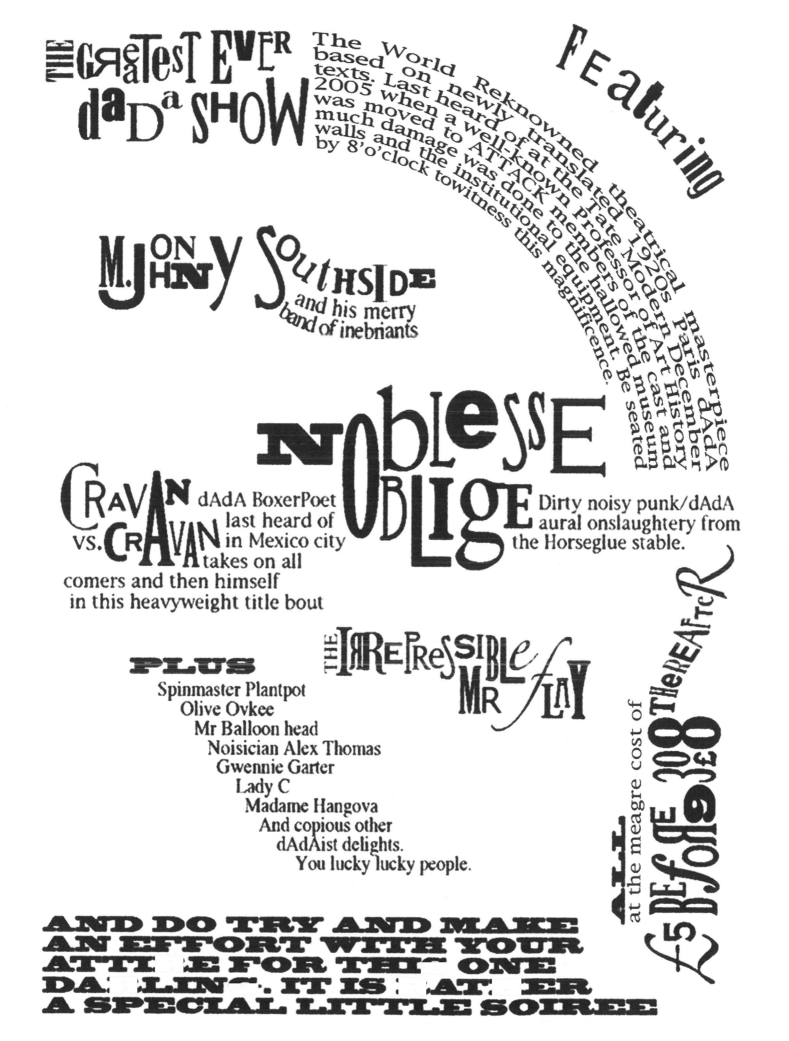

THE GREATEST EVER dADa SHOW

The World Reknowned theatrical masterpiece dAdA based on newly translated 1920s Paris December 2005 texts. Last heard of at the Tate Modern of Art History. was moved to ATTACK members of the cast and much damage was done to the hallowed museum walls and the institutional equipment. Be seated by 8'o'clock to witness this magnificence.

Featuring

M. JOHNNY SOUTHSIDE
and his merry
band of inebriants

NOBLESSE OBLIGE
Dirty noisy punk/dAdA
aural onslaughtery from
the Horseglue stable.

CRAVAN vs. CRAVAN dAdA BoxerPoet
last heard of
in Mexico city
takes on all
comers and then himself
in this heavyweight title bout

THE IRREPRESSIBLE MR FLAY

PLUS
Spinmaster Plantpot
Olive Ovkee
Mr Balloon head
Noisician Alex Thomas
Gwennie Garter
Lady C
Madame Hangova
And copious other
dAdAist delights.
You lucky lucky people.

ALL at the meagre cost of £5 BEFORE 8 £6 THEREAFTER

AND DO TRY AND MAKE
AN EFFORT WITH YOUR
ATTIRE FOR THIS ONE
DARLING. IT IS AFTER
A SPECIAL LITTLE SOIREE

Klub Dada

The greatest ever Dada
show is in town:

'Try and make an effort with
this one darling, as it is a
rather special little soirée.'

On the night, a clairvoyant,
her pet ventriloquist and
Mr Balloon Head entertain.

Dada is a spoon, Dada is
a chair, Dada is a club.

www.theatreoftheabsurd.co.uk

KLUB DADA

GREATEST EVER DADA SHOW

In this, the nintieth year since the discovery of the dADa spirit, Madame Bombador and her troop of DadA beauties regail your ocular and auricular orifices with performances based on freshly translated 1920s Paris daDA texts. If your behinds are not firmly planted on the turqoise leather glory of the Mad George's upholstery by HALF PAST EIGHT you will have the great misfortune to miss this wonderous spectacle.

JOHNNY SOUTHSIDE & his Merry Band of Inebriants

GOLDEN ROCK ORGANIC fuKING
London's Fucking Burning

JOHN COOPER CLARKE

The MaN FROM URANUS

Bard of Beasley Street

TURN COMMERCIAL RD

CABARET PISS
Dancing, shouting and pissing all over the heads of the fun starved bourgouisie

PSYCHIC TWINS Have they a message for you?

Admission can be yours for a mere FIVE POUNDS before 9 8 THEREAFTER OAPS GRATUIT

PLUS
Frau Weisleitner
The Shellacs
The Weeping Saw
Mr Balloon Head
Olive Ovkse
Pig Porn Merchant
Madame Hangova Psychic
Dadafication Beauty Salon
And Copious other
dADaist delights

AND DO TRY AND MAKE AND EFFORT WITH YOUR ATTIRE FOR THIS ONE DARLING, IT IS RATHER A SPECIAL LITTLE SOIREE

SIGN OF THE TIMES
PRESENTS
SCANDAL!
SATURDAY
APRIL

SIGN OF THE TIMES
PRESENTS
SCANDAL!
SATURDAY 2ND APRIL
(9:30-3:30)
D.J.'S:
MARK MOORE
SABRINA DUNCAN
FINBAR
CHILO
FASHION SHOW
GOODNIGHT
COLLECTION BY **JOIE**
CABARET FROM
Kentucky Fried Scandal

189 REGENT$ ST.

lurid
scandal probe
often obscene
from VICE
Yum Yum!
Randy To!
arty Girl
lurid
sex lurid
scandal probe
MPs often obscene
Wipe sneers from VICE

HARD ROCK/HEAVY METAL
BAND

SEEKS GUITARIST AND DRUMMER
WE PLAY COVER SONGS FROM;
AC/DC,IRON MAIDEN,METALLICA
JUDAS PRIEST,GUNS N ROSES ACCEPT
DEEP PURPLE,THIN LIZZY
WE ALSO WRITE OUR OWN SONGS
WHICH WE TAKE OUR INFLUENCES FROM ABOVE.

IF YOU ARE INTRESTED IN THIS TYPE OF MUSIC,
PLAY AN INSTRUMENT AND WANT TO JOIN A BAND GIVE US A
CALL
BRIAN   PAUL

DICE CLUB

WETDOG
Vile Imbeciles
Eve Black/Eve White
Plus DJs
THE JUNKETTES
HEIDI HEELZ   Mr PHIL G

SUNDAY 9th DECEMI

7PM - LATE! AT THE LEGION, 348 OLD STREET
ENTRY: £3 PLUS ROLL DICE TO WIN SHOTS
www.myspace.com/diceclublondon

GUNS
other bands

PLACE:
Project Orange
DATE:
15th Dec 2007
DOORS:
8pm- LATE
ENTRANCE FEE:
£4/£5

Project Orange, 43 St. Joh
Directions: from Clapham
towards high street, Tu
& it is on

DICE CLUB

DICE CLUB

NEILS CHILDREN
Hatcham Social
Burning Idiot Noise
Plus DJs:

FFIN JOE   HEIDI HEELZ
ENA Zoo Music   Mr PHIL GOOD

DICE CLUB

SUNDAY 12th AUGUST

THE HORSE & GROOM
(28 Curtain rd, Shoreditch EC2)

Playing Live:
THE NUNS
ddd
project:KOMAKINO
Electricity In Our Homes

DJs:
The She Set
Heidi Heelz
Jon Slade

UNDAY 11th NOVEMBER

DICE CLUB

DICE CLUB

DAY 9TH SEPTEMBER:

ATHS CLASS
ntitled Musical Project
w Black Light Machine

Js Coffin Joe and Heidi Heelz

AY 14TH OCTOBER:
HE VIOLETS

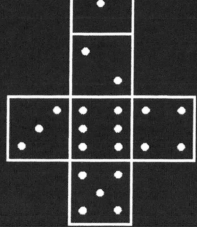

The Violets' Single Launch

The Violets
The Guillotines
Ipso Facto

DJs
The She Se
Coffin Jo

Dice Club

In Spite of Earthquakes ... Roll the Dice!
Heidi runs Dice Club. Dice Club is special.
Manifold sets of carved dice flutter across
the flyer like moths, their formation
punctually changing with each new night.

For this book, I picked up lots of Dice Club
flyers and stuffed them in my pocket.
Later, I laid them out on the floor,
oscillating patterns all around me.
Varying graphic shots to the head:
black, white and deadly.

DICE CLUB

DICE CLUB

The Violets' Single la

The Violets
The Guillotines
Ipso Facto

SUNDAY 17th

ENTRY: £3 PLUS ROLL DICE TO
7PM - MIDNIGHT AT THE LEGION
www.myspace.com/di

DICE CLUB

"...let the dice decide. Indecisive? Uncertain? the rolling ivory tumble your burdens away."

The Dice Man by Luke Rhinehart

ing LIVE:

OYS OF BRAZIL

ONE MORE GRAIN

MUPRHY'S MAYBELLENE

DJs: HEIDI HEELZ

THE SHE SET

AURORA

Thurs 31st May

BRAND NEW AND RETRO ALTERNATIVE NEW WAVE ROCK N' ROLL DISCO!

LIPPY

THIS WEEK - FRIDAY 28th JULY

THE YELL (marquis cha cha)

punky funky 'gang of four, the rapture and the Fall' all in one 6 piece package. Recent single "my baby's into witchcraft".

EVERY FRIDAY at the ROYAL VAUXHALL TAVERN

10PM - 2AM.   FREE B4 11PM.   £5 AFTER.
RVT HAPPY HOUR 8-9PM

DJs LUSH and *SPARKLE*

LIVE BAND at Midnight every Week

RVT 372 Kennington Lane SE11   www.myspace.com/lippyclub

21

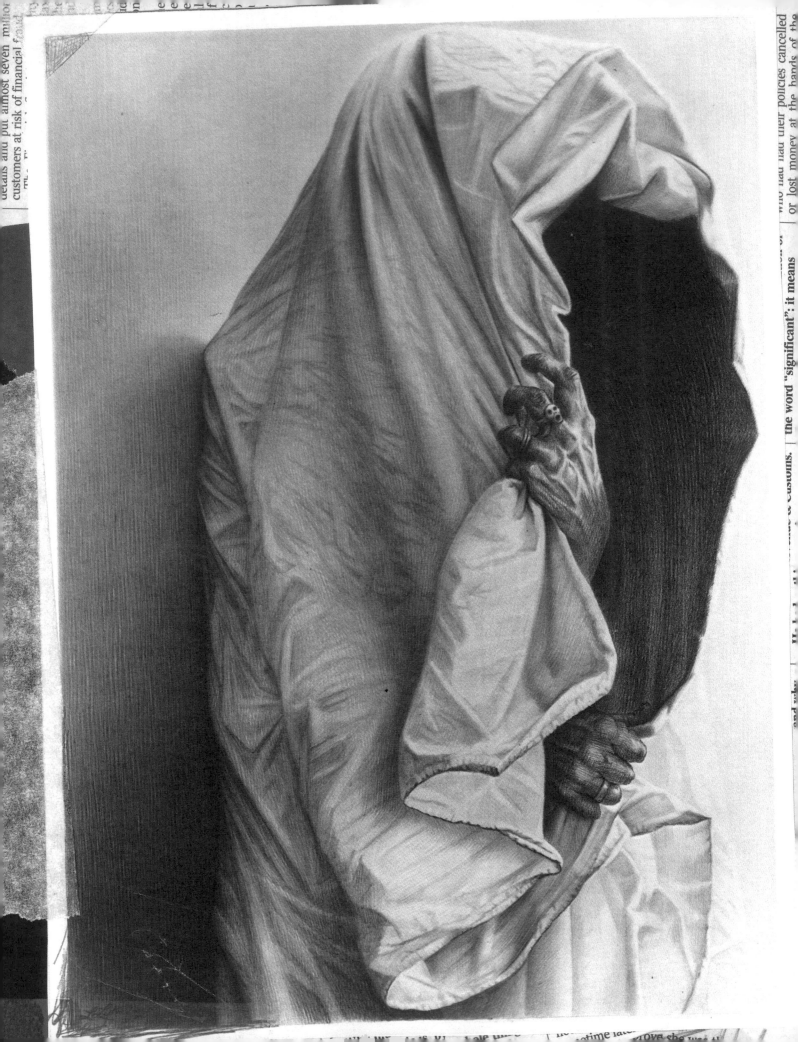

Kaos

The Wonder and Horror of the Human Head

Kaos stages underground parties.
I've collected the flyers for a while.

One of them shows a pencil-grey spectre,
another a hoard of skeletons and horrors.

Unhinged! Mirrors, cloaks and rattlesnakes.

Kaos flyers are speedy flights to the
underworld, they rub the back of your
neck and make the dark sparkle.

24

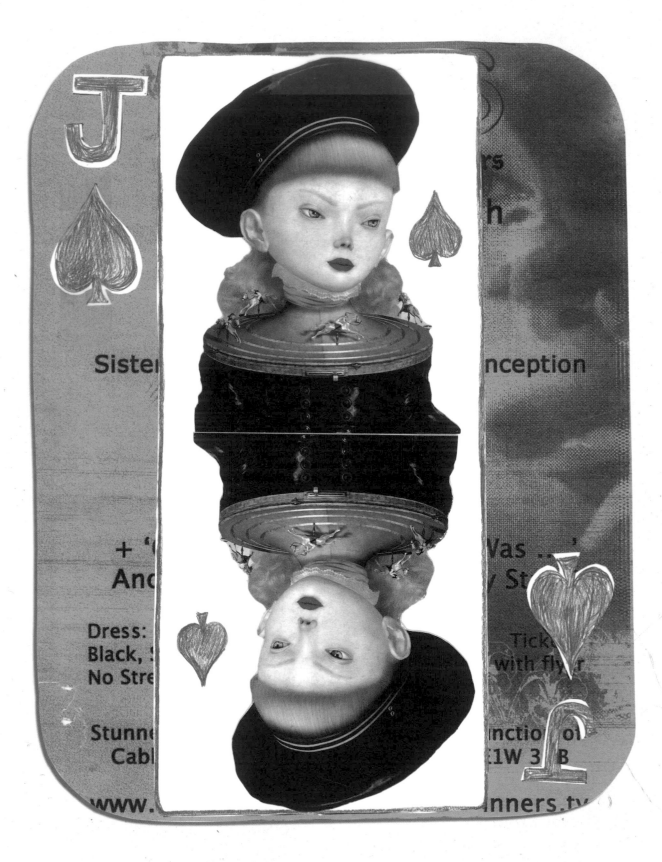

The Loving Nightmares

Live at Gossips,

Dean Street, London,

Friday 3rd January 2003,

Onstage 10pm £5

Your Hosts
MAX and AL

28

happy friday

5

SEA FUCK SCROLLS

DEAD SEA FUCKIN SCROLLS

grind

Bored? Broke? ....then why not come to

HAIR + HEELZ

Saturday 17th June at The Penthouse

25a belfast rd london n16
(nr to stoke newington station)

www.myspace.com/comfortandjoy

norway noisarek

fivequid

The Bonanza Country Revue
@ The BirdCage
Sun 2nd Sept '07

Live Acts
**Michael J. Sheehy
& The Hired
Mourners**
+
Christopher Rees
(album launch)
+
Bonanza Dj set:
Country, Blues
& Swamp

...e, 58 Stamford Hill, Stoke Newington, N16.

Café Bo
Plug
on

Free Ent
6pm-10.3
(1st band 7p

[cafe bar plug -ton- cul] gets cosy with
HOMOCRIME

**Saturday 24th April 2004
At The Poison Club
(aka The Chinaman)
52 Dalston Lane
8pm 'til late late late**

LIVE BANDS
Linus, The Cherrybombers

**VEGAN
FOOD**

HOMOCRIME DJs

30

**More details soon at
www.homocrime.org
and 07949 976 016
(Queeruption hotline)**

FILMS

£4/£3

---

april fools trio

Canyonesque, Psychadelic
...mmond, electric guitar, drums
...ute, sax and vocals.
Paul Moss, Steph D'Silva
and Thomas White.

Red
Rose Club
seven sisters
road, N7

Genre-hopping, soaring,
soothing   grooving electric
free spirited folk meets POWER
TRIO!
meets improv-Funk + blues

...day 14th January 2007
doors 8pm   £5 on door   £3·50 concessions

...w.myspace.com/aprilfoolstrio

Sunday June 12
2pm - 6pm
£3 w/flyer,
£2 concs

The Pleasur...
Bethnal

FANZINE

A Fanzine for the Big Cats

Boy George

Billy Mackenzie

Iggy Pop

David Bowie

Marc Bolan

Dusty Springfield

Kate Bush

Fanzine is for the fans. I went to one in the name of Kate. The flyers are fanzines; the night is the 3-D, chromatic, stereophonic version. Fans circle and fandom goes berserk.

I'm a fan of Marcus who runs the night. His flyers are dedicated to everyone's favourite pop kittens. Here is a one-off Fanzine flyer, specially made for my journal.

At home, I have pinned my Fanzine flyers to the bedroom wall.

They are pink mostly, with lots of photocopy blocky choppy black, copies of copies, names of names, all cut and paste. Cut this out ... paper homages to the big cats.

Club Disaster

Miss Fortune, Lady Havoc. Paris is burning!

There is DIY disorder everywhere. The tape has unravelled, the milk has spilt and Club Disaster is to blame.

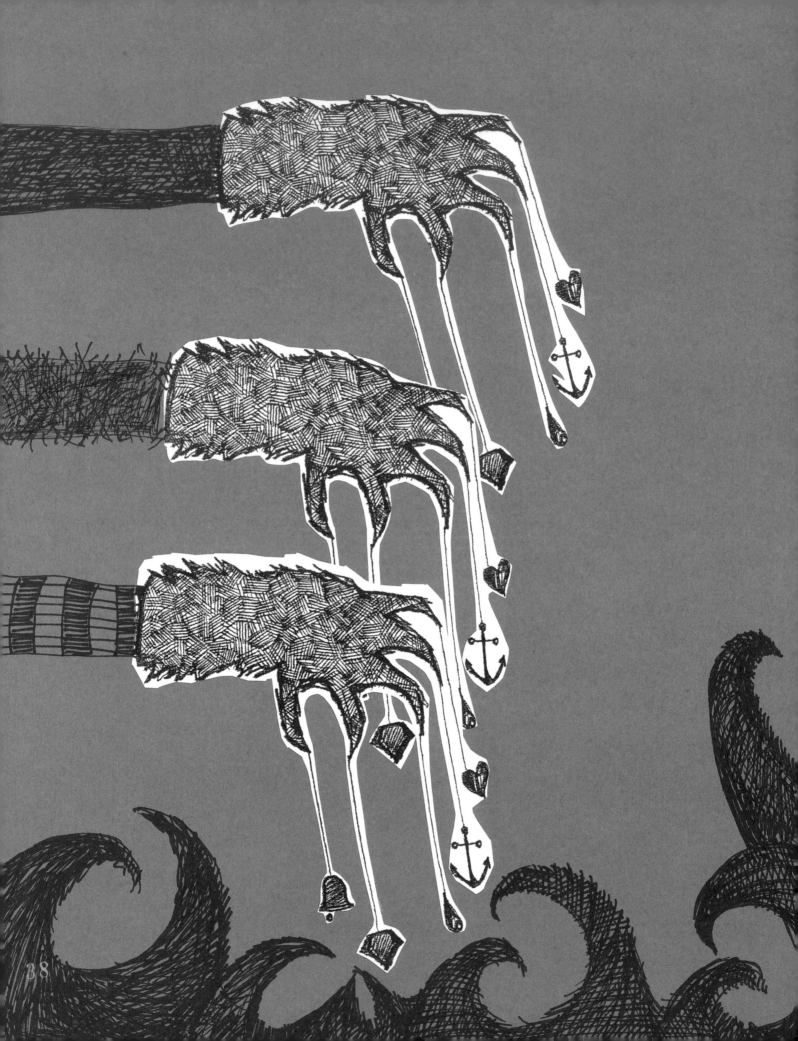

40

HE WAS BORN WITHOUT A
HEART. SO, HEARTLESS, HE
ATE HIS PARENTS WITH NO
FALSE START.

HE BORE TWO GREAT HORNS
AT THE TOP OF HIS HEAD.
"GRIM AND GLORIED" THE
WOODLAND ANIMALS SAID.

~~WILE~~
WHILE ANOTHER DREARY NIGHT
PASSED, A GIFT WAS LEFT IN
HIS CLASP.

FROM NOWHERE THE PACKAGE
CAME, BUT A GRACEFUL LACE
RIBBON SMILED AT THE GAME.

THE SADISTIC
TALE OF THE MUTILATED HEART
by KEZ GLOZIER

Unskinny Bop

This one's for you, Thunderthighs!

Snacks!

Badges!

All time Top 10 Podge Pop anthems!

Limbo!

For hefty ladies, fat fags and all their friends

A special disco nite on Friday 2nd August   10pm-late

Dance to the sound of the fat underground, plus soft rock, crisco disco and garage punk hits

Upstairs at Sahara Nights (formerly the Liquid Lounge), Pentonville Rd, Kings Cross

42

Free entry - priority entry with Ladyfest pass / flyer

ANTISOCIAL

Antisocial and Buster Bennett

Buster Bennett made this picture, a faithful homage to Jean-Paul Goude and Grace Jones. It spreads to the bleed and tickles and kicks.

DAN & RICHARD PROUDLY PRESENT:

GOLF
SALE

**EVERY SUNDAY 7PM - 11.30PM,
HOXTON BAR (BACK ROOM),
HOXTON SQUARE.**

**RESIDENT DJ'S PLUS WEEKLY
SPECIAL GUESTS;**

**FEB 1ST: HOUSE OF JAZZ
FEB 8TH: PAM HOGG
FEB 15TH: QUEENS OF NOIZE
FEB 22ND: PING PONG BITCHES**

46

TRANSGENDER ✦ TRANSGRESSION ✦ TRANSMUTERS
TRANSSEXUAL ✦ TRANSCONTINENTAL ✦ FETISH SEX THRILL CULTS

CLUB WICKED, 4 TOOLEY STREET, LONDON BRIDGE SE1
9PM—6AM E-MEMBERS £12, DOOR £15; £12 ADVANCE FROM PARADISO, SOHO
DJS: PANIC (SLIMELIGHT, PERVERSION), BATON SINISTER, STUNNERS
EMAIL US TO BE INCLUDED ON OUR CONFIDENTIAL MAILOUT OR FOR A LIST OF NEWSGROUPS
GWENDOLINE@LISTHOUND.COM HTTP://GWENDOLINE.NIXNET.COM

GWENDOLINE EVENTS PRESENTS

THE ADVENTURES OF STUNNERS

SATURDAY 31 MAY 2003

23rd JULY
We Smoke Fags
Niyi
P-i-X
at DURRR

Rory Phillips
The Lovely Jonjo

27th August
Voxtrot
Live at
DURRR
4.8

Rory Phillips
The Lovely Jonjo
Our Man Fred

The End
West Central St. W1
10pm - 3am   £4/6
www. durrr. co.uk
myspace. com/durrrclub

9th July
Barringtone.
at Durrr
Rory Phillips
The Lovely Jonjo
Our Man Fred
The End
West Central St.
10pm ~ 3am
£fire/six
www. durrr. co.uk
myspace. com/durrrclub
myspace. com/i-am-gina

P-i-X
†HOLY HAIL   11TH JUNE
AT DURRR

Durrr replaced Trash

Hand-drawn crisp oblongs
of delight, these flyers
go out weekly.

Here is the Lovely Jonjo
and there is Princess Julia.

Durrr flyers are always
original and special.

Delicate, tangly illustrations of the
gangly creatures from Durrr.

THE STICKS PEAS

BRIGHTON! HIDEOUS TOURRENT
OF ROCK N'ROLL PARTY NUMBERS!

TEMPERATURES
LONDON!! SEARING ABSTRACT FREE DRONE ROCK!

LONDON! MIDDLE EASTERN CLATTER AND TWANG!

WED
15TH
AUGUST

ISAMBARD
KINGSTON BRUNEL
LONDON! TAPE! MINIDISK! & GUITARS! NOISE MANIPULATION!

THE POOL BAR
104-108 CURTAIN RD, OLD STREET

FIVE POUNDS. 8PM.

MYSPACE.COM/CHAOSVCOSMOS

CHAOS VS COSMOS PRESENTS

53

54

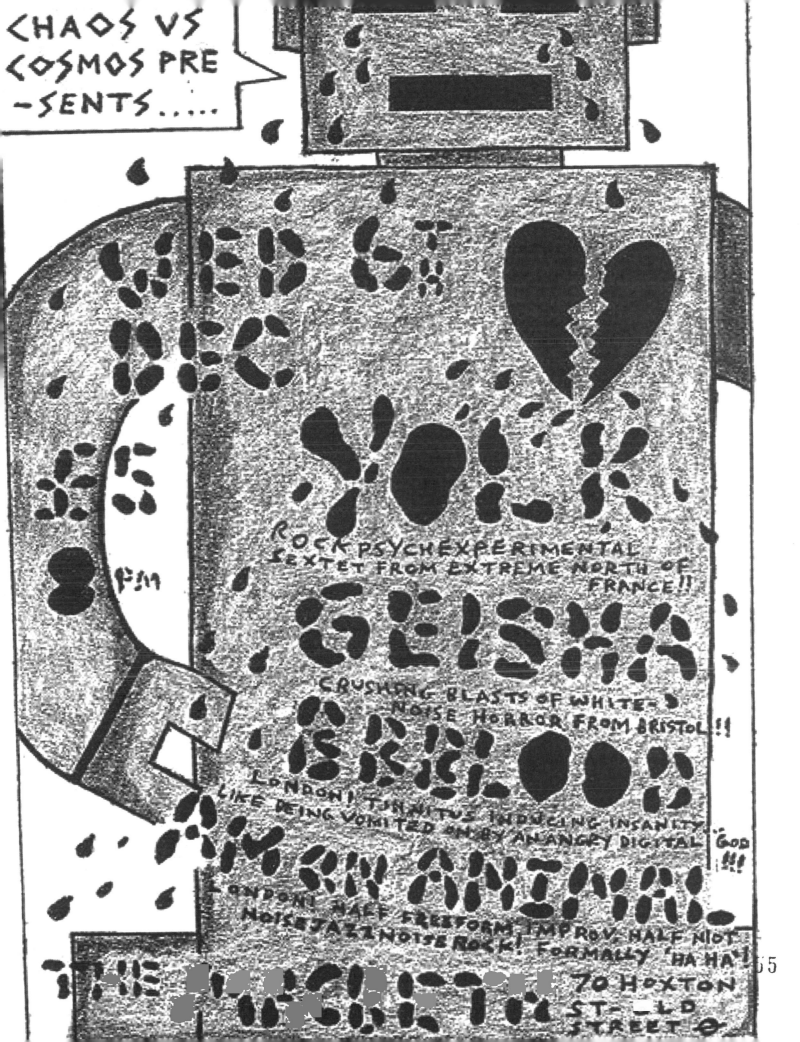

57

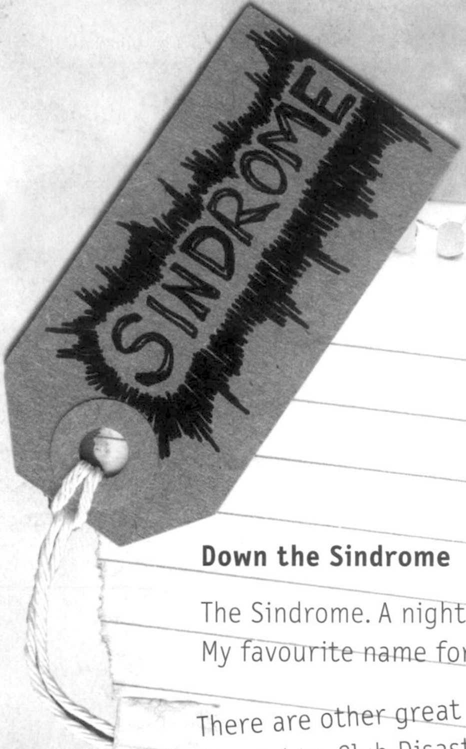

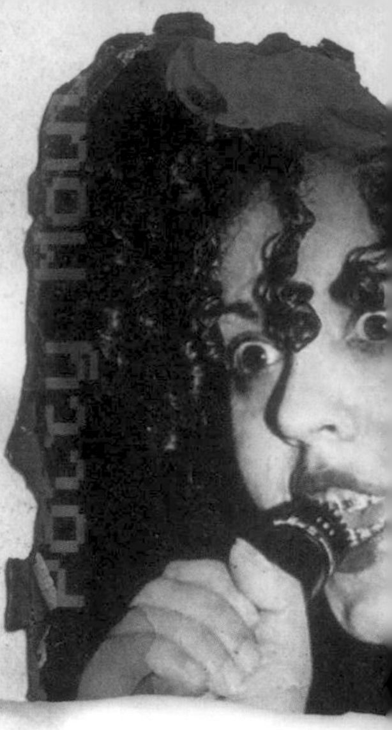

Down the Sindrome

The Sindrome. A night for sinners.
My favourite name for a night.

There are other great names
for nights: Club Disaster;
Club Wotever; Magic Poison;
The Beautiful Bend; You Me
Bum Bum Train; Dice Club;
Durrr; and Club Cellophane.
I could go on.

IT'S THE NEW THING

Upti ght has m ov ed... ....

DOWN THE SINDROME

Every Wednesday

itch at The Polar Bear, 30 Lisle St, China Town

nd I don't give a damn 'bout my reputation
Never said I wanted to improve my station
And I'm only doin' good
When I'm havin' fun
And I don't have to please no one'- Joan Jett

Daughters of the Kaos
and very special guests
play

RiotRapBitchLektroPopKitschRocknRoll
ock - Lights - ys and girls ood vibes

st Out Presents...

iRL FRIDAY
the 13TH

en SPECIAL

ry DRINKS
ry GIRLS

es
STREET
ate

THE HEAVY LOAD CLUB

61

JUNK

JUNK
ARE FREE ADOLESCENTS

To Hell with Junk

Junk club was hard, tight and in Southend – underground in the Royal Hotel basement.

It is no longer, you missed it.
'I was there.'

So were: Neil's Children, The Violets, Pink Riot, Snow White, The Horrors, The Errorplains, Wretched Replica and These New Puritans. Disjointed post-Punk Electro Pop Disco No Wave Noise.

A lightning bolt on the front of the flyer screams 'Junk'. Ciaran did the flyers. I have so many of them; the graphics are caustic, they bite.

JUNK JUNK JUNK JUNK

SATURDAY 6TH MAY//////////////
JUNKCLUBS SYMPATHETIC ORCHESTRA PLAY
THE FINEST IN GARAGE ROCK ELECTRO P
DISCO PUNK AND NO WAVE NOISE>>>>>

RAGE ROCK
ECTRO POP
CO PUNK
WAVE NOISE

OZO! UPSTAIRS IN THE MA
EE ENTRY. CHEAP DRINKS.
S WITH GUEST CORPORA

JUNKCLUB.

unk SATURDAY 10th APRIL
. ROYAL HOTEL. 1 HIGH ST. SOUTHEND

CO PUNK NO WAVE NOISE ELECTRO POP GARAGE ROCK

OLIVER VON BLITZKRIEG
SPIDER WEBB

JUNK CLUB
JUNKCLUB
SATURDAY JUNE 3RD 2006

THE SEXBEAT GIRLS

SEXBEAT

AT MOTHER BAR
LOST PENGUIN
PROJECT KOMAKINO
— IPSO FACTO —
ANIMALS OF FARTHINGHOOD
PLUS SEXBEAT DJ's
£5 FOR SEXBEATNIK'S
FRIDAY AUG 10TH 2007

SEXBEAT

HAVE IT ALL

SUN & MOON
SPECIAL EDITION

31st July 04

Magic Poison: On the Rocks

Half Tesco Disco, half Boombox, so the hacks have said, though the flyers are something else.

Sophie Thunder does most of them, most of the time.

Painted magic and tasty poison, watch your socks when you are On the Rocks!

MAGIC POISON

MAGIC POISON

Rock n' Roll Electric Gla...
Come one, come all...
Thursday 9th Augu...
Live dj sets fro...
The Thunder Sister...
Special Guest dj Sam...
of Trafalgar...
Fashion showcase of de...
Becky Raa...
Performance piece...
Poison's Paul...
at On The Rocks, 25...
Shoreditch...
9.30 -
£4 before 11pm, ...
Dressing ...
"There is no terroris...
anticipa...
- Alfr...

MAGIC POISON

Sophie Thunder '07

Stil
late...

mail:LonelyHeartsAreGo@hotmail.com

(next to Highbury + Islingte

+VERY
SPECIAL
GUESTS+DJ's
PLAYING
heartbreaking punk
new wave, 60's pop
+ rock'n'roll! 73

£4 w/flyer, 5 without

CHERUBS

£1

Sophie Thunder

@ the lanery...

Ms Thunder's drawings are sharpest black on A3 white and are formed as crisply as snow. She maps the flyer with an image of a girl and then writes all the important stuff around her head in her own hand.

'Tap n Tin, last Thursday of every month.'

The flyers came to me as originals, large format, like posters.

Sophie photocopies them down. Image incised, text drawn, speedily photocopied and safely kept: a 'Sophie Thunder time capsule'.

80

the beautiful bend

presents

Tennessee Waltz

Shrimpers Cove

Scat On A Hot Tin Shoe

Silence In Courts

thursday 7th july

10.30   till   3am

entral station

7 wharfdale road

ings cross

IN THE NIGHT

5 INCH HEELS for the FIRST TIME!

81

di harvey

The Beautiful Bend

The Beautiful Bend

I like Donald's flyers for the beautifully named The Beautiful Bend.

He ran the night with Sheila Tequila. On the flyer they describe it as a jazz-house, pool-house, smoke-house, shag-house, booze-house, nut-house.

Wow.

PIQUE

ON SATURDAYS EVERY WEEK STARTING SATURDAY 17TH FEBR

AT CLUB EXTREME, GANTON STREET, (OFF CARNABY ST), W1

10 till 3 (£3/£5)

DONALD URQUHART

Donald Urquhart

Donald Urquhart draws lines of efficiency. He is with a big gallery now, but he used to create flyers with Antonio Lopez for Matthew Glamorre's infamous night, Pique.

Fine, dry lines he draws, fine faces, fine characters, double figures, singular creatures, girls from films. They bang.

I'd like to own one of his drawings, but for now I have this snowy white-and-black flyer.

BLAME MATTHEW GLAMORRE AND DONALD

PIQUE

SATURDAY 17 FEB.
and every week

PIQUE:
PIQUE:

CECILS, NEW ROTICS,
Dirty Old Dress-Ups,
GUTTERATI, He-Shes,
TROMPE LOYALS, the
deeply over-dressed

stompe, sulk, sneer
fume, flounce, nettle

WE WANT WINNERS ON AN
EGO TRIP, NOT LOSERS ON
A LOVE DRUG

MATTHEW GLAMORRE AND DONALD , MUSIQUE MAGNIFIQUE 10-3 (£3/£5)

CLUB EXTREME, GANTON ST. W1 (OFF CARNABY ST.).

PIQUE

85

AT EASTER

WED. APRIL 11th LIVE ON STAGE AT 12.30

MATTHEW GLAMORES

PRESENTS

EXTAVA PERFORMANCE

TEMPO TEMPLE

"YOU SNAKE ... ... LL YOU
ESC...

ORIGINAL SOUNDTR... ... CRAWFOR...
PHOTOGRAPH... ...KER.

BLESSINGS TO - Andy Lovegrove, S... ...nchita Scott, Tessa Hallma...
...nna Minauge, Link Leisure, Darryl, And... ...Billy, Josh & Babs, Domani
Mark Goghety, Guy Beckett, Billy, L... ...The Dancers, Popata,
Kerry & Phiona, Adele & ... ...Rythm King.

DEDICATED T...

DJs COLIN FAVER, L... ...REVOR FUNG,
JEFFREY HINTON... ...HOBART.

Matthew Glamorre is Shocking!

Matthew Glamorre was once going to put on a night called Shocking. In the last twenty years he has put on many nights, though Shocking was one that never happened.

Matthew gave me a sketch for the Shocking flyer. 'IT'S ELECTIC HECTIC!' it screams. Welcome to Glamorre world.

Matthew has years of club flyers in a box under his bed and they tell a different story of London – they give us an alternative history. He likes the fact that I'm trying to revise our histories with my book.

Matthew's nights are legendary, his flyers incendiary. M. Glamorre the visionary, helping me with my revisionist history.

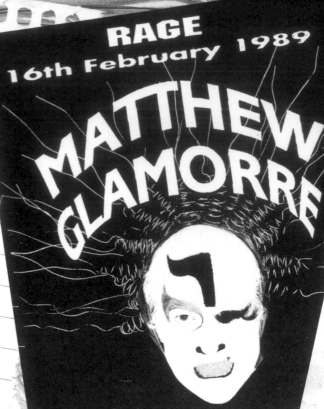

RAGE
16th February 1989
MATTHEW GLAMORRE
presents The Stage...

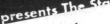

MATTHEW GLAMORRE
PRESENTS
HIS BIRTHDAY
IN ASSOCIATION WITH DEBZ
11 – DAWN
FRI AUG 11
45 DERBYSHIRE ST E.2.
STICTLY INVITE ONLY – LAST TILL DAWN
WEAVERS FIELDS.
BETHNAL GR.
DERBYSHIRE ST.
BETHNAL GREEN RD.

Matthew Glamorre
Presents a Fashion Show of

LIMPIDS AND ARIAS

So The City Slept On Through It's Own
...y, Adoring Relics From Glories Past...
...A Temple To Nostalgia In The Place Of
Things New...

...ere Is Beauty In Deformity But It Is An
Acquired Taste

...OME BEHOLD THE FACE
OF THE FUTURE

Thursday June 9th 1988

LIMELIGHT

136 Shaftesbury Avenue

Doors Open 9.30 p.m.

Fashion Show On Stage At Midnight

Special Thanks To:

...ayben, Max Jaquard, Rod James, Sybil Rouge,
...Weinreb, Club Studios, Corinna Sargood, David
...aret, Claudia Bliss, Jane, Ben Kendrick, Nicky,
...ok, Morag, Melanie, Gill Cataclysm, Nostalgia,
Mark, Sharon, John Smith.

DJ: Adam Jessop
Photography: Tessa
Choreography: Clive
Original Soundtrack: Neil Kaczor

...erson For You And A Guest With This Invitation
£7 Per Person Without

This Invitation Cannot Be Sold Or Transferred
...ght Of Admission Reserved/Capacity Is Limited
Proof Of Age May Be Required

BE...
THE FACE...

30

RETRO HETRO HOMO
BEATNIK PEACENIK
LOVENIK HATENIK
A TEACHER A PREACHER
A CREATURE FEATURE
RARE GROOVE FONKY
A ROOM FULL OF PEOPLE
STUCK IN A TIME WARP..
..... AGAIN

SOHO BOHO NO HO (PERS..
HETEROPHOBIC HOMOPHOBIC
RACIST SEXIST AGEIST
TRASHY TACKY WACKY
SMACK CRACK MATT BLACK
A RAGGA A BLAGGER
A SOCIAL LADDER

IS

SMaShling

SWING BEA
MINCE
LENNY
LENNY
LENNY

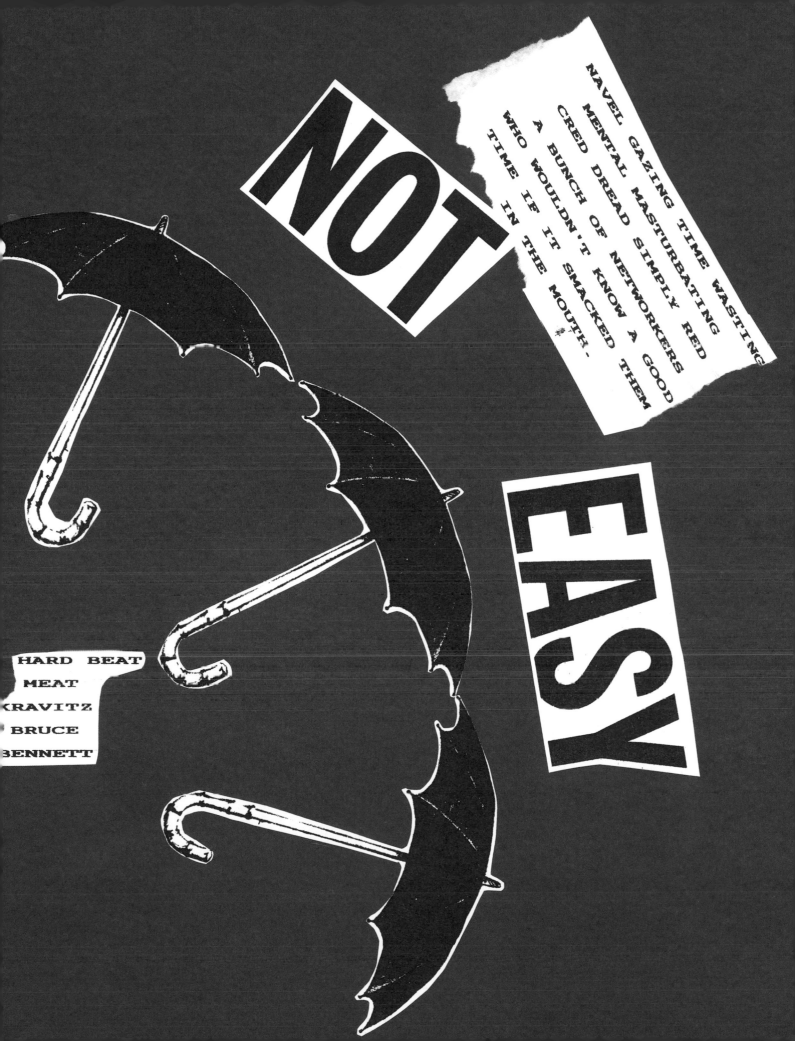

Wolfgang Tillmans
Princess Julia
at the Cock

special **Cock** DJs
Wolfgang Tillmans
Princess Julia

The Cock

at

Ghetto
Falconberg Court
Soho (behind Astoria)

4 April 2003

£5 with flyer/ before 11:30/ £6 after

Wolfgang Tillmans

It's The Cock on a Wednesday night, playing for all those insolent, cock-sure boys and girls. 'The Cock is in association with *Butt* magazine this week.'

Wolfgang Tillmans photographed and designed the flyer for it. Terrific, it's another favourite that I'll keep forever.

Thrillers, bodice rippers, romantics, a thousand of them crowd together at The Cock, chattering and dancing under the keen lens of Tillmans.

Wolfgang is a winner of the Turner Prize, and his lovely flyer is in my book. I'm thrilled.

Wolfgang Tillmans
AT "THE COCK"

Motherfucker

SAT 28 APRIL @ BARDENS BOUDOIR   LIVE MUSIC FIRST
38-44 STOKE NEWINGTON RD, DALSTON   THEN SUPER FUN DANCE
8PM-2AM £4 BEFORE 9, £6 AFTER, OR £5 FLYER   PARTY AFTER!
ARRIVE EARLY   BEFORE 11AM
FUCKERS!

songs! songs! songs!   LIVE! LIVE! LIVE!
ROUND TABLE   PARTYLINE
KNIGHTS   FEAT. ALISON BRATMOBILE. PUNK POP RIOT GRRL!
BOLT ACTION FIVE   BEST FWENDS
SOUNDSYSTEM   DORKY TEXAN DUO DO RETARDED ANTI POP
LADIEZ DI (E)   WE SMOKE FAGS
DAUGHTERS OF THE KAOS   ELECTRO SKUNK ROCK YEAH!
                         TROUBLE V GLUE
                         ITALIAN ELECTRO DUO

every 2nd + 4th SATURDAYS OF THE MONTH (TIL BURNOUT)
WWW.CLUBMOTHERFUCKER.COM

'KEEPING THINGS FOUL MOUTHED & FUTURE FACING FOR
THE PAST FOUR YEARS' - THE GUARDIAN

Saturday 10th September
Upstairs @ The Garage
9pm-3am
£4 before 10 flyer/NUS
£5 after innit

'The night that unites London's most foul mouthed and deep'
- The Guardian

club **Motherfucker live!**

CANTANKEROUS

TWISTED FERAL PUNK
ROCK ELECTRONIC
FUCKERIES

Motherfucker
Motherfuck

+ support.
arrive early fucker

Motherfucker – Daughters of the Kaos

Daughters of the Kaos – our saviours from dreariness – play music. They also put on a night called Motherfucker, and it runs at Bardens Boudoir in Dalston.

Our descendants of mayhem conceived of their night on the night bus.

Collaged chaos in Tipp-Ex and pink; black drastic marker pen requests we be punctual.

Starts at eight, eight-thirty is early enough. Tonight: Chris Vodka, Lauren Flax, Electralane, plus Rhythm Kings, Kasms and Noisy Pig.

www.clubm...

...ry & Islington tube

club Motherfucker

SAT ... 07

DIY

FO'S EARLY
GORE
FUCKER

deck
selection
courtesy of:
ALLEZ-ALLEZ
NO BRA
LADIEZ DK(E)
plus hosts/fuck ups
♥ DAUGHTERS OF THE KAOS

SECRIT
WE WOULD
KILL U IF WE
NAME ONE OF OUR
FAVE BANDS

ShitDisco
Superspecial
guests

ALSO PLAYING LIVE!!!

GROVESNOR
ELECTRO SOUL & THE MODERN METROPOLITAN
FROM EX-HOT CHIP DRUMMER ROB

MACromantics
KILLROCK STARS SIGNED, FORMER GUITARIST
OZ'S MOST EXCITING HIPHOP
FROM GEN ELECT STAR

KAPUTT
ICE COOL INDIE
WITH HOT, HOT
PASSION FROM
EX-GO TEAM
DRUMMER SILKE

CLUBMOTHERFUCKER.COM
AT BARDENS BOUDOIR 8PM-2AM £4 B49 E6
38 STOKE NEWINGTON RD, DALSTON £5 FLYER
LIVE MUSIC FIRST, THEN SUPER-FUN DANCE PARTY AFTER!

Motherfucker

LIVE! LIVE! LIVE!
TETINE
SILICON VULTURES
THE FLESH
THE ARCADIA PARTY PROGRAMME

TUNES! TUNES!! TUNES!
MICPROBES
(RUFFCLUB NYC)
TAPEDECK
BASEBALL FURIES
LADIEZ DI(E)

PLUS
HOSTS/
FUCK UPS
DAUGHTERS

SAT 9 JUN
GARDENS
BOUDOIR

38-44 STOKE NEWINGTON RD
DALSTON, 8PM-2AM, £4 b4 9, £6 AFTER

CLUBMOTHERFUCKER.COM

Trademark

Trademark made flyers for Trade and for Heaven. They are famous, graphic and great.

I treasure these flyers that look like old *Interview* covers. They are images that pop with colour and fizz with fervour. They make me smile.

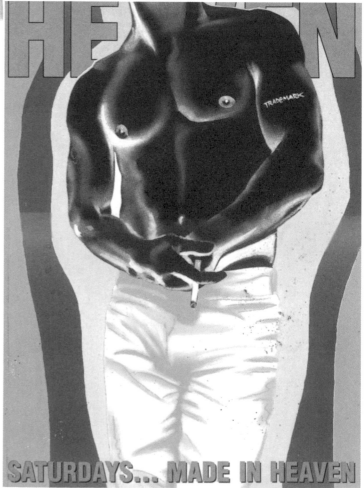

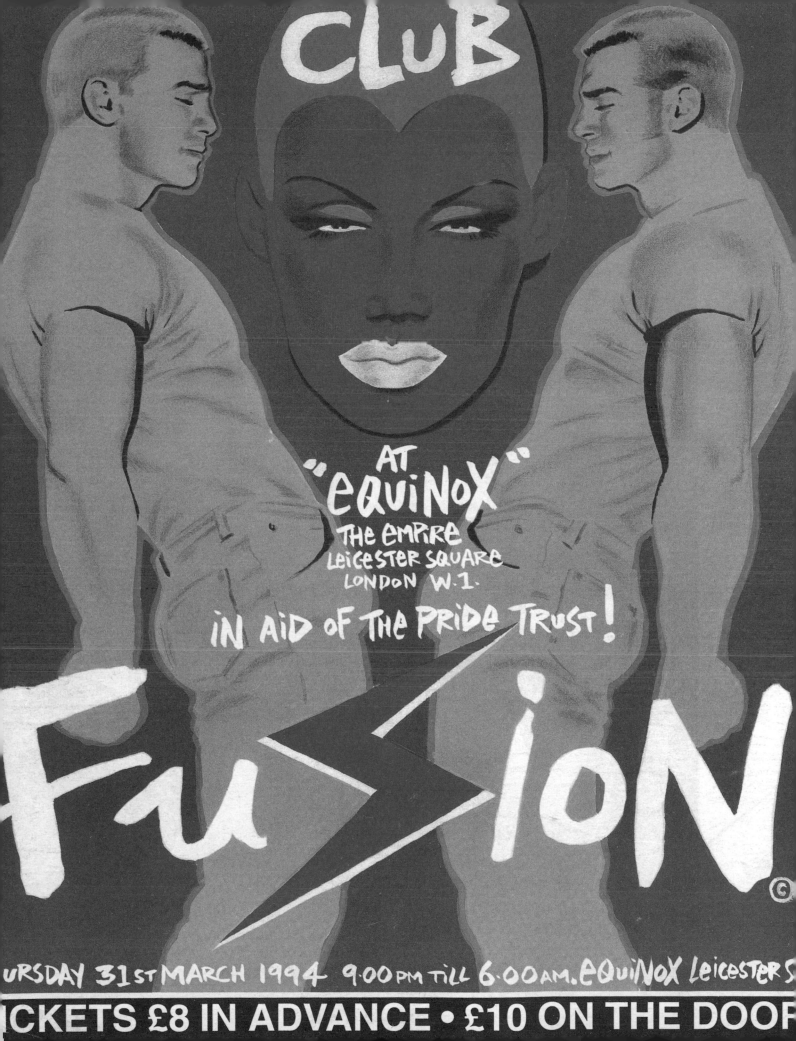

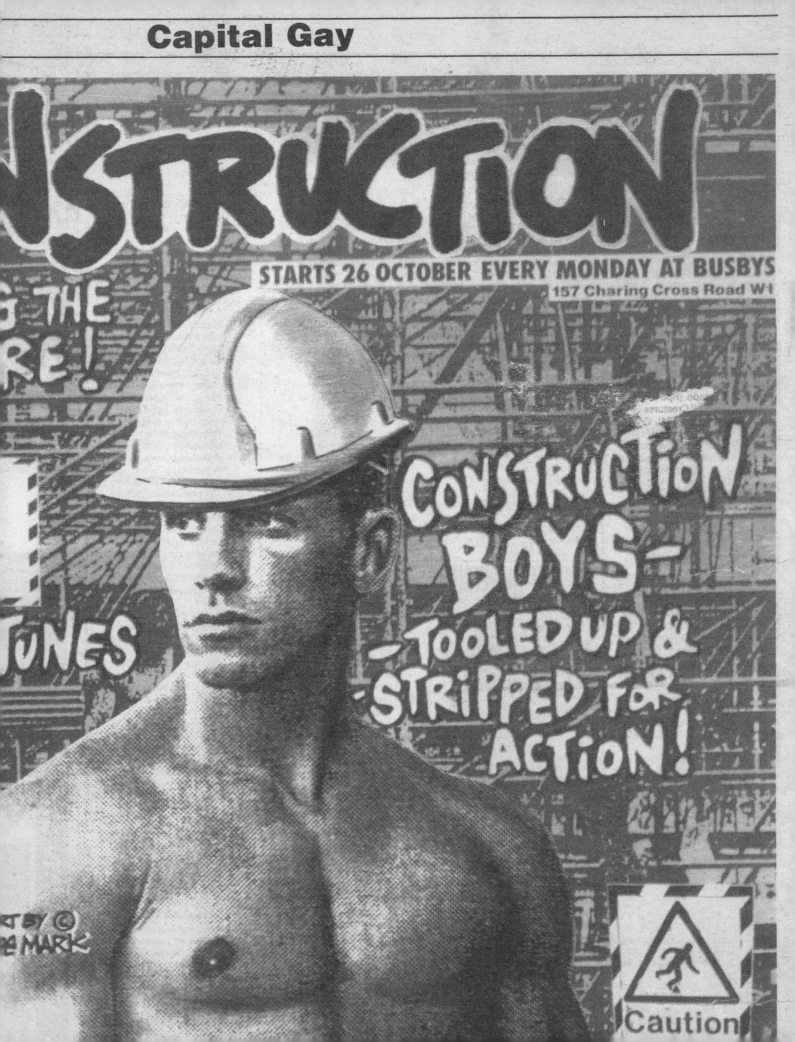

Pissed Futurist   Frantic New ...om

MATTHEW GLAMORRE   DAVID C...

ALL OVER MY FACE

CRIMP, BACKCOMB, SPRAY AND DRY – GET THAT LINER IN YOUR EYE

FOR ONE NIGHT ONLY

MAQUILLAGE

FRIDAY 8th OCT. '83

HASH 11
11 WARDOUR STREET W1.

£5

YOU BETTER LOOK GOOD

WE DO!

DJs

Michael Mascara Murph
Richard Crimper Torr
Tim Tweezer Wheeler

Live on Stage

New Individualist
KERRY SHAW
Numanoid Dance Duo

INE BELL CHIME LIP LINE GOO

she just blew up   heidi heelz miss pain

DANCE DANCE DANCE   DANCE DANCE DANCE

DANCE DANCE DANCE

DANCE DANCE DANCE   DANCE DANCE

KLING KLING

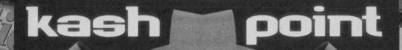

No.1 Static
Gypsydelica
October 8pm til 2am
DIR 36 STOKE NEWINGTON RD
LONDON N16
£8 after

rocksteady roots & ska from
No.1 Station
turntable vagabonds...
GABONDBOOGALOO

NEW WAVE ELECTRO
BANDS AND DJ'S
FREE ENT

MIDNIGHT

kash point
luminous   *amphibious*

Club Wotevere

CUT N PASTe
Music for your aural delectation

Tamla Motown
45 RPM
MADE IN GT BRITAIN
TMG 690
DON'T KNOW WHY I LOVE YOU
STEVIE WONDER

BOY, DANCING SPOT.
rsday Starting 16th November 2006
Bar, 8 Denmark St, WC2
Jonjo (Trash)
n To Zai)
FREE !Dance!
!Dance!Dance!
DANCE
DJ'S on Rotation
BOY, DANCING SPOT.

ery Saturday night 7-11 @ First Out, St Giles High St. WC2H 8LH, Tottenham Court Road Tube

You Me Bum Bum Train

It's 'All aboard the Bum Bum Train! Buckle up and soak your under-carriage.'

I live just a fifteen-minute bus ride from the Old Ship pub where Bum Bum parks most weeks.

Kate and Morgan run the night and they make smashingly dazzling artwork for their flyers. They are surreally dreamy and terrific.

Dance to Soul/Swamp/Surf/Girl Group/Gypsy. Sometimes they have a karaoke. A karaoke, raggaoke, jokeoke, hokekoke, socklimbooke, danceoffoke, or so it says on the flyer.

I called Kate and Morgan the other day and they both said that their mums are pleased.

YOU, ME, BUM-BUMOKE TRAIN

22ND JUNE
8PM – 2AM
BETHNAL
GREEN
WORKING
MENS CLUB

KARAOKE
RAGGAOKE
JOKEOKE
HOKEOKE
SOCKLIMBOOKE
DANCEOFFOKE

BUMBUM
£7 £6 WITH FLYER
9TIL2

SUPRIS

THE BETHNAL GREEN
MENS CLUB
POLARDS ROW

DONT TELL ANY
WW.BUMBUM.COM

AT DURR
THE END
18 WEST CENTRAL ST.
WK1A 1JJ
10PM – 3AM
£4/6

DURR.CO.UK

122

The Artists

Artists' names appear in *italic*. Their work has sometimes been commissioned for individual promoters and/or club nights and venues.

Rhiannon Adam: Life 58; *Gina Barber*: Chandra Haabjeern at Durrr 48–49; *The Beat*: The Beat at The Macbeth 98; *Theres Bergman*: First Out 60–61 / Cut'n Paste at First Out 112–13; *Zena Blackwell*: Potty Mouth 60–61 / Club Motherfucker 99–107; *Kate Bond* and *Morgan Lloyd*: You Me Bum Bum Train 114–23; *Ray Caesar*: Lee Adams at Kaos 23–27; *Marilyn Coleman*: Virginia Creepers 8–9; *Lavinia Co-Op* and *Sheyla Baykal*: Installations Instillettos 8–9; *Zac Ella*: Sexbeat 66–67; *Matthew Glamorre*: 2XS 8–9 / Tempo Temple 86–87 / Rage, Shocking and his birthday party 88–89 / Limpids and Arias 90–91 / Smashing 92–93 / Kashpoint 112–13 / Maquillage 112–13 / Bishi 112–13; *Kez Glozier*: Kez 38–41; *Wayne Gooderham*: Uptight 60–61; *Keith Grant*: Down the Sindrome 60–61; *Pablo Guez*: Sun and Moon 69; *Gwendoline Events Presents*: The Adventures of Stunners 46; *Heidi Heelz*: Dice Club 16–19; *Jonjo*: Hot Boy Dancing Spot 112–13; *Steve Keane*: Pre, Gremlin, Pseudo Nippon and Gentle Friendly 34–35 / Chaos Vs Cosmos 53–57; *Kling Klang*: Kling Klang 112–13; *Laurie Lipton*: Lee Adams at Kaos 21–22; *Alex Long*: Unskinny Bop 42–43 / Ghost School 45; *Antonio Lopez*: Matthew Glamorre at Pique 84; *The Loving Nightmares*: Live at Gossips 28; *Harry Malt*: Wonderful Bastard 8–9; *Benjamin Marra*: Clive Kelly at Computer Blue 50; *Max Mason, Kirsten Glass, DJ Lush*: Lippy 20; *Craig McCarthy*: Bistrotheque 94–95; *Danilo Milic* and *Richard*: Golf Sale, 45; *Jane Moore*: Julie Fogarty's Dirty Ticket 45, 68; *Charlie* and *Zara Morris* aka *DJ Pineapple* and *DJ Ra*: Club Disaster 36–37; *Ciaran O'Shea*: Spunk at Junk 47 / Junk 65 / Experimental Circle Club 112–13; *Ben Palmer*: Immoral Minority 8–9; *James Priestley and Secretsundaze*: All Over My Face 112–13; *Andrew Quinn* and *Patrick Duggan*: This is Modern Love 112–13; *Marcus Reeves*: Fanzine 33; *Ruaidiri*: Le Vagabond 112–13; *Ruth Russell*: Homo Bop and Homocrime 30–31; *Jonna Saarinen*: Midnight to Six 112–13; *Scottee, Buster Bennett & Simian Coates*: Antisocial 44; *Aric Shunneson*: Juggernut 34–35; *Johnny Southide*: Klub Dada 10–13; *Liam Sparkes*: Trencher 29, 51, 62–63 / Trencher at ICA 52 / Magrudergrind Yacopsae 59; *Steady as She Goes*: The Plank 45; *Sophie Thunder*: Paul Pierrot-Joyce at Magic Poison 70 / 33145 Junkies 71 / Buffalo Bar 72–73 / Tap n Tin 74 / Spring Arts 75 / The Dragon 76–77 / Sophie Thunder 78–79 / Cherubs and The Delaners 80; *Wolfgang Tillmans*: The Cock 99; *Trademark*: Village 8–9, 108 / Heaven 108 / Equinox 109 / Construction 110–111; *Donald Urquhart*: Scandal 14–15 / Hair + Heelz 30–31 / Beautiful Bend 81, 83, 84, 85; *Veris*: House of Wrong 64; *Thomas White*: April Fools Trio 30–31; *Robert Whitmore*: The Heavy Load Club 60–61; *Daniel Wilson*: Helen Gee at Death Party 30–31; *Spencer Woodcock*: Ishmael Sykes at The Boat 96; *Wotever World*: Club Wotever 112–13.

I dance therefore I am

Acknowledgments

Thank you to all my friends and family.

I would like to thank all the artists, in particular: Zena Blackwell, Kate Bond, Matthew Glamorre, Heidi Heelz, Morgan Lloyd, Ciaran O'Shea, Paul Pierrot-Joyce, Sophie Thunder, Wolfgang Tillmans at Maureen Paley, Marcus Reeves, Trademark, and Donald Urquhart at Herald St. I am also grateful to Bistrotheque for their assistance.

With special thanks to: Rhiannon Adam (for design and illustration), Jamie Camplin, Johanna Neurath, Daniel Norton, Julia MacKenzie and Susan McCarthy.

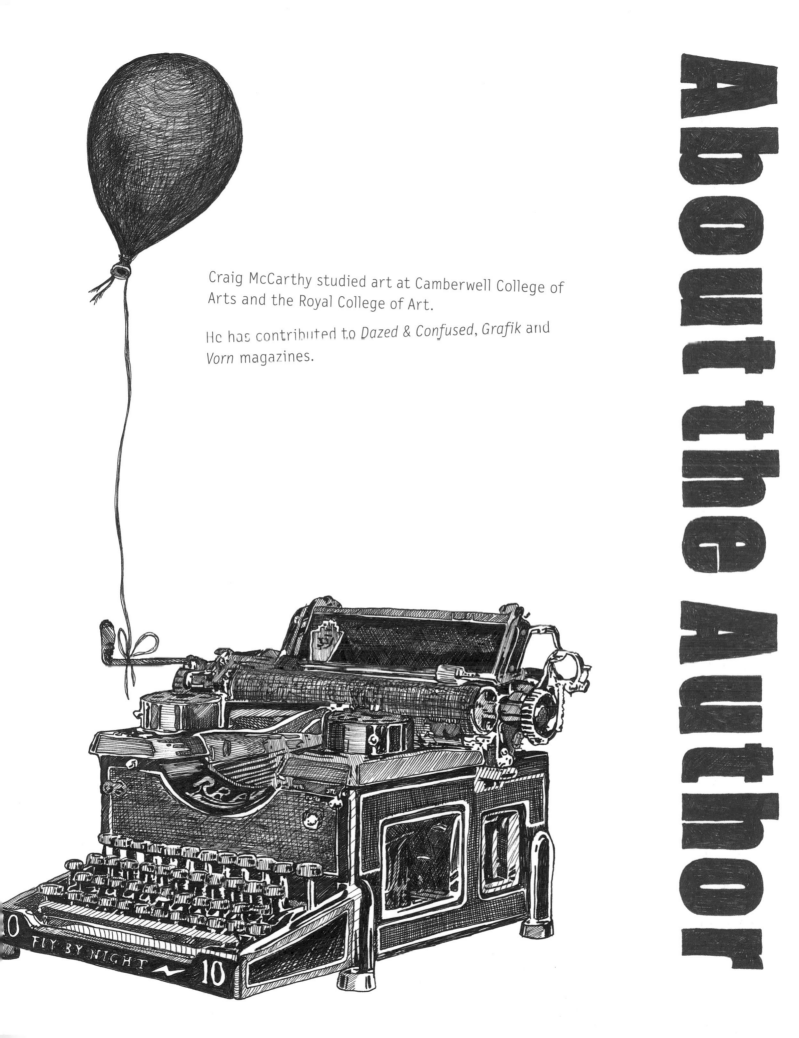

Craig McCarthy studied art at Camberwell College of Arts and the Royal College of Art.

He has contributed to *Dazed & Confused*, *Grafik* and *Vorn* magazines.

About the Author